NOW SHOWING

MATILDA

CHARLIE AND THE CHOCOLATE FACTORY

REVIEWS OF TWO ROALD DAHL BOOKS AND THEIR MOVIE VERSIONS

by Cynthia Swain
illustrated by Regina Dueno

Table of Contents

Book/Movie Reviews

What is a review?

A review is a text that evaluates a work of art, such as a book or movie. In a review, the reviewer, or critic, describes what happens and shares opinions about it. The critic discusses what is good or bad about the book or movie. The critic also makes sure to add many details to support his or her opinions and judgments.

What is the purpose of a review?

Many people want to know about a book or movie before they read or see it. People want to know what the story is about and if it is "right" for them. Is it exciting? Are the characters interesting? A review helps people decide whether to take the time to read a book or to buy a movie ticket (or rent a DVD).

Who is the audience for a review?

When an author writes a book, he or she has an audience in mind: people who are interested in the subject of the book. When a critic writes a book review, he or she is writing to those people who might want to read the book being reviewed.

Often, popular books are turned into movies. Will the movie capture the same feeling that made the book a success? The audience for a movie review is anyone who is curious about a movie, including fans of the original book. Moviemakers, however, frequently change the plot of a book. And remember that movie advertisements don't give an objective opinion about how good or bad the movie is.

The review title is catchy and gets across the reviewer's general opinion.

The review identifies the intended audience.

The review includes a summary.

The review includes the reviewer's judgments and compares the book and movie.

Features of a Book/Movie Review

The book review gives information about the book and author.

The review evaluates the book and movie, identifying strengths and weaknesses.

The review concludes with a question or statement that tells what the reviewer thinks.

The movie review names people who made the movie.

How do you read a review?

Pay attention to the plot, characters, and the subject matter. Ask yourself, *Would this story interest me? Did it interest the reviewer? How can I tell?* Think about the reviewer's judgments and how the reviewer rated the book or movie. What did the reviewer like and dislike? Did the reviewer have good reasons for his or her opinions? After you read the review, ask yourself, *Do I want to read the book or see the movie now?* If you have already read the book, ask yourself, *Did the reviewer like how the filmmakers turned the book into a movie? Will I?*

TOOLS FOR READERS AND WRITERS

Writer's Voice

When your friends call you on the phone, can you recognize their voices? Each voice is distinctive, just like each friend's personality. Writer's voice is no different. Everyone's writing is different from everyone else's. Every writer chooses certain topics, selects certain words, includes certain details, and uses a certain style and mood that makes his or her writing as unique as a fingerprint. Good writers use their voices to add feeling to their writing. Good writers also adapt, or change, their voice for different audiences and purposes. For example, you would use a different voice to write an e-mail to your cousin inviting him to your soccer game than you would use to write a letter to your principal requesting a field trip for your class.

Suffixes

Good writers use as few words as possible to convey meaning. One way they accomplish this task is by using suffixes. When suffixes are placed at the end of a root or base word, the meaning of that root word changes. For example, the suffix **-y** means "being or having." Instead of saying "being like fruit," authors say **fruity**. Instead of saying "having sun," authors say **sunny**.

Compare and Contrast

To add more depth and detail to stories, authors often compare or contrast information, showing how things are similar or different. Many times, authors use certain words and phrases to indicate a comparison or a contrast. Comparison words and phrases include **along with**, **similarly**, and **as well as**. Contrast signal words and phrases include **although**, **on the other hand**, and **either . . . or**. Other times, authors compare and contrast without using signal words and phrases.

ABOUT THE AUTHOR

Roald Dahl

A fighter pilot, a spy, and a famous author—Roald Dahl led a fascinating life. He was born in Wales, Great Britain, in 1916, though his parents were originally from Norway. His father died when he was young, but his mother kept the family in Britain. It was his father's wish that Dahl be educated in British schools.

Dahl was a very brave man. During World War II, he joined the British Royal Air Force and flew many missions in Africa. Once his plane crashed and he became blinded. But he recovered his sight and went on to fight in many battles. He also served as a secret agent during the war and gave key information to the British government.

Dahl's career as a writer began in 1942 when he was asked to write about his war experiences for the magazine *Saturday Evening Post*. After that, Dahl continued to write short stories for adults. He began to write children's books when he started to make up bedtime stories for his daughters Olivia and Tessa. His first children's book, *James and the Giant Peach*, was published in 1961. In addition to that book, he also wrote, among others, *Fantastic Mr. Fox, The BFG*, and the stories reviewed here: *Matilda* and *Charlie and the Chocolate Factory*.

Dahl's children's books are often funny, but they are not lighthearted, happy stories. In fact, he was a master of dark humor. He wrote clever, witty stories about tough situations, such as the terrible poverty of the Bucket family in *Charlie and the Chocolate Factory* or Matilda's thoughtless parents and cruel headmistress. But in each book, the hero overcomes all odds and wins in the end.

In 1953, Dahl married a famous actress, Patricia Neal, and they split their time

Dahl with his wife, the Oscar-winning actress Patricia Neal

between the United States and England. He did a lot of his writing in a hut in his garden in England, writing his books and stories by hand with a pencil.

Roald Dahl died in 1990. He is considered one of the greatest children's writers of all time.

BOOK REVIEW:

Matilda Saves the Day!

Poor Matilda! Her father and mother treat her like a scab that should be picked off and flicked away. Worse, an evil headmistress who is out to get little kids rules Matilda's school. But don't feel too bad for Matilda. She may be misunderstood, but she outsmarts everyone.

Matilda, a children's book by British author Roald Dahl, was published in 1988. It's a story about an unhappy genius trapped in a rotten family. It shows how you can turn your life around, no matter how tough it is.

Dahl makes fun of just about everybody, but adults get the worst of it. Matilda's parents are utterly awful. Matilda's father

violates the law by selling used cars that break down as soon as they are driven off the lot. Matilda's mother leaves her alone all day while she rushes to her bingo games. Each night, the whole family has to sit in front of the "boob tube." And dinner consists of warmed-up frozen meals.

If anyone could be worse than Matilda's parents, it is the school's headmistress, Miss Trunchbull. She was once an Olympic athlete. Now she is just deranged!

Dahl paints her vividly with words. According to him, Miss Trunchbull looks like someone "who could bend iron bars and tear telephone directories in half." In school, she uses her strength to throw helpless children out the window. Or she punishes them by locking them in a tiny cupboard with sharp glass on the walls called "The Chokey." Not surprisingly, she terrifies everyone. She would **terrify** me, too. Miss Trunchbull is completely insane. She definitely deserves to be locked up.

The only nice adults in this novel are the librarian who befriends Matilda and her first teacher, Miss Jennifer Honey. Miss Honey is kind to everybody, but she doesn't have any backbone. She's afraid of Miss Trunchbull and can't stand up to her, though I can't say I blame her! Miss Honey also lives in a tiny house that is like a prison. There is no heat or kitchen. There is hardly any food. The house has wooden boxes for furniture. Why can't Miss Honey afford to live in a nice house? That's one of the key mysteries in the book for readers to solve.

I liked the children in this book, especially Matilda. First of all, she is off-the-charts smart. She teaches herself how to read. She does complicated math problems in her head. She's even blessed with a special ability to move things with her powerful mind.

Second, no one displays more **bravery** than Matilda. She's not afraid to go out on her own to the library. And she stands up to her nasty, **sarcastic** father. She has the guts to teach him a lesson every time he's mean to her. For example, on one occasion she smears superglue in his hat. Another time, she secretly pours hair dye into his shampoo so his hair turns a weird color. She even hides a talking parrot in the chimney so her parents think they hear a ghost in the house.

Matilda is a terrific book. It teaches readers a valuable lesson. So what if you come from a terrible home? You can summon the power inside yourself to make things better. That's what Matilda does. She comes up with a secret plan to save the day. When she goes into action, everybody is shocked and stunned, especially Miss Trunchbull. There's nothing better than seeing the headmistress more frightened than the children she tries to scare! Read the book for yourself and see. As far as I'm concerned, everyone should read *Matilda*, even—or maybe especially!—adults.

MOVIE REVIEW:
Matilda the Magnificent

How often do you see a movie and think the book is so much better? The entire time you're wondering what happened to the character or scene you loved. Why isn't it in the movie? Or the movie is so bad that you either fall asleep or you get up and walk out. Well, you won't have to worry about all that with the movie version of *Matilda*. This movie really delivers!

Roald Dahl's book is a modern children's classic. Matilda is a misunderstood genius who lives in an awful family and goes to a terrible school. Screenwriters Nicholas Kazan and Robin Swicord are pretty faithful to Dahl's story in their 1996 movie. But they also add a little magic of their own! The result? An even better movie script. More about that later.

Hats off to Danny DeVito, the director and one of the lead actors. He's brought a great cast together. He and his actress-wife, Rhea Perlman, play the parents of Matilda, and they are **hilarious**. They dress like clowns, eat like pigs, and care only about themselves. Take note of how the director makes sure there are a lot of close-ups of these two actors. The looks on their faces will make you laugh every time!

One of my favorite scenes happens early in the movie. Matilda is a newborn. Her father is leaving the hospital with

her. He holds her baby car seat as if it's a garbage bag. Even funnier is that when the family arrives home, both parents get out of the car and forget the baby's even in it. This scene was not in the book. Still, it brilliantly **dramatizes** the utter abandonment Matilda feels in **childhood** from the day she is born!

Pam Ferris plays the cruel and **abusive** headmistress of Crunchem Hall Elementary School, Miss Trunchbull. Remember this actress? You probably saw her in one of the *Harry Potter* movies. She played the insulting Aunt Marge, who one day goes too far and makes Harry really mad. He uses magic to blow her up like a balloon, and she just floats away.

As Miss Trunchbull, Ferris turns herself into a frightening

headmistress. She's massive and ugly. She carries a horseback-riding crop to scare everybody. She hates everything about kids and can't wait to punish them. She locks Matilda in her horror chamber, "The Chokey." The reason? Matilda's dad, a used car salesman, sold her a "lemon."

Mara Wilson plays Matilda as a nice kid but no pushover. When her father is mean to her, she strikes back. One night, Matilda's dad is so angry with his daughter for reading books and not watching TV that he grabs her head and forces her to watch. But Matilda has her revenge. She uses her special mental powers to make the TV explode. This is another scene that should have been in the book but wasn't.

That's why this movie is one of my favorites. Matilda is a take-charge kid! She realizes her parents aren't really going to do much for her. She doesn't cry about it. She just goes her own way and has fun.

Danny DeVito Rhea Perlman Embeth Davidtz Pam Ferris
and Mara Wilson
ROALD DAHL'S

Matilda

A FILM BY
DANNY DEVITO

A little magic
goes
a long
way…

From the author of "James and the Giant Peach"

In one scene, Matilda makes her own pancakes. I'd be afraid to do that because it might turn into a disaster. But maybe I should try new things, like Matilda!

The screenwriters weren't afraid to take chances, either. They added two major subplots to the movie. A subplot is a small addition to the main story. It adds more scenes to enhance the character or action. The first subplot is about a pair of goofy undercover FBI agents watching Matilda's home. Her parents are clueless that they're being watched day and night. The agents want proof to bust Matilda's father for his shady used-car business. Matilda warns her parents, but do they listen?

The second subplot involves Matilda getting revenge on Miss Trunchbull. She creeps into Miss Trunchbull's home and fixes it so the headmistress thinks her house is haunted. The next day, Matilda not only uses her powers to write a ghostly message on the board, she also makes two erasers attack Miss Trunchbull. Then the other kids get in on the action. They give the headmistress a send-off she will never forget.

As great as this movie is, it should come with a warning. Small children may find it scary to see how badly Matilda's parents treat her. And there is a lot of violence involving the sadistic Miss Trunchbull.

For those old enough to take it, don't wait another minute to see this movie on video or DVD. This is a film you'll want to watch over and over. You'll have a good laugh at these funny actors and enjoy how Matilda becomes a real-life superhero!

Understand the Reviews

- What book and movie are reviewed?
- Look at the book review of *Matilda*. Does the critic like the book? How can you tell?
- What does the critic think you can learn from reading *Matilda*?
- Look at the movie review of *Matilda*. Does the critic like the book or the movie better? How can you tell?
- The critic cautions young viewers in the movie review. Why?

Focus on Comprehension: Compare and Contrast

- How are Miss Trunchbull and Miss Honey different?
- In the second review, the critic contrasts the movie and the book. What are some differences?
- In the second review, the critic compares herself with Matilda. What does she want to change about herself?

Analyze the Tools Writers Use: Writer's Voice

- On pages 8–9, the critic uses the words "deranged" and "insane" to describe Miss Trunchbull. What picture do you see in your head when you read those words?
- The critic explains why she likes this book by using organized thoughts. What does this tell you about the critic?
- Both articles are written in a light mood. What examples from the articles prove this?
- In the second review, the critic says that she wouldn't make her own pancakes because she might make a mess. Then she says she might try. What has the critic learned from the movie?

Focus on Words: Suffixes

Make a chart like the one below. For each word, identify its part of speech. Then identify the base or root word and suffix. Finally, identify the word's meaning.

Page	Word	Part of Speech	Base or Root Word	Suffix	Definition
9	terrify				
10	bravery				
10	sarcastic				
12	hilarious				
12	dramatizes				
12	childhood				
12	abusive				

BOOK REVIEW:
Charlie the Champ!

Charlie and the
Chocolate Factory

Roald Dahl

Roald Dahl's most famous book of all has got to be *Charlie and the Chocolate Factory*. The book, published in 1964, is about a boy with one simple wish: to see inside the mysterious Willy Wonka Chocolate Factory.

The story is based on Dahl's experiences growing up. Dahl was miserable at his boarding school. But there was one happy memory he never forgot. In the 1930s, the chocolate company Cadbury sent candy to his school for kids to test. That inspired Dahl to write this book.

Charlie Bucket, the book's hero, has little going for him. He and his family live in a broken-down house. They have only one bed. Charlie's only escape and inspiration are Grandpa Joe's fascinating stories about Wonka and his factory. According to Grandpa Joe, one day Wonka got so sick and tired of spies trying to steal his candy ideas that he closed the factory. Then, suddenly, the factory reopened. But who works there now? Why are there never any workers going into or out of the factory?

All these mysteries are about to be solved. Willy Wonka is holding a worldwide contest. He has hidden five golden tickets in candy bars. Those who find the golden tickets will get a tour of the factory. They will get a lifetime supply of candy, too. Charlie is the last of five kids to find a golden ticket.

19

In my opinion Willy Wonka is very, very strange. He's superpolite and dresses like an announcer in a big-top circus. The book describes him as "quick and sharp and full of life." But as he takes the winners on their tour, you can tell that he's not a big fan of most children or their parents. I suppose it's not hard to see why. Charlie's fellow ticket winners are **obnoxious**. Augustus Gloop eats all day. Veruca Salt is spoiled beyond belief. Violet Beauregarde just wants to chew gum. Mike Teavee is obsessed with watching television. Wonka takes care of them one at a time. One gets sucked up into a vat. Another becomes a giant blueberry. One more goes down a garbage chute. I have to admit, though, that I was sorry to see them go. They were extremely funny characters.

Charlie, of course, doesn't meet their fate. That's because he's a good kid who listens to what Wonka says. It's hard not to **sympathize** with Charlie, but I have to admit I found him a little too good to be true. He's an angel compared with the other ticket winners, and no child is as perfect as Charlie—no child *I* know, at least. Dahl seems to want us to believe that good wins over bad every time. That may be true in this book, but I'm not sure it's true in life.

Dahl's message may be overly **optimistic**, but his imagination is still spectacular. I loved his description of the factory's chocolate river with funnels to make fudge. The trained squirrels cracked me up when they snapped open all those perfect nuts for the candy. But a warning: Don't step over the line with squirrels because they'll get back at you.

Think all that is incredible? How about candy traveling by air signals to your very own TV? And nothing is more fantastic than the tribe of the Oompa-Loompas. Not only are they hard workers but they also sing hilarious songs each time one of the bad children gets thrown out of the factory.

Read this book to find out what happens to Charlie Bucket. Enjoy Dahl's magic, but don't get fooled by it. Sadly in real life, there would be no golden ticket for little Charlie.

In the reviewer's opinion, the magical elements are among the book's strengths; the overly optimistic message is one of the book's weaknesses.

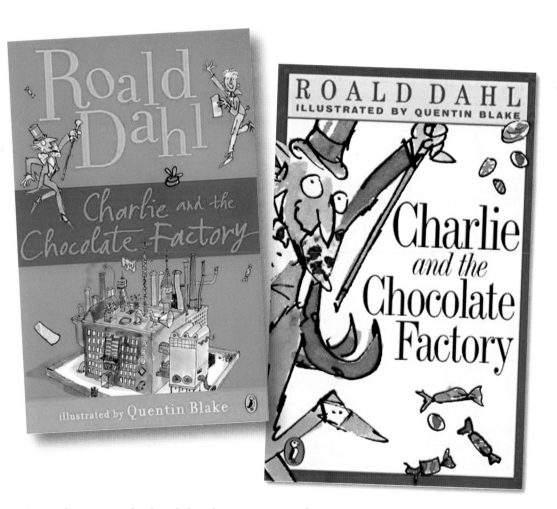

Over the years, the book has been reprinted many times, often sporting a different cover.

MOVIE REVIEW:

Charlie Is Way, Way Over the Top

The reviewer gives the movie review a catchy title and makes it clear that, in her opinion, the movie is not very good.

Readers can tell from the reviewer's "voice" (writing style) that she was excited to see the movie, which was based on a book. Note that she refers to the movie's director and the main actor, key people to include in a review.

The reviewer provides a brief summary of the movie plot. Fans of the book in particular will want to know how the book and movie compare.

I couldn't wait to see the movie *Charlie and the Chocolate Factory*. I liked the whimsy of the book, but I really liked director Tim Burton's other movies. *Batman* and *Planet of the Apes* were great. And Johnny Depp is one of my favorite actors. He was brilliant as Jack Sparrow in the *Pirates of the Caribbean* series. I thought he would be an amazing Willy Wonka in the 2005 movie. There were also supposed to be interesting additions to the book's plot and dialogue. But when I saw the actual movie, it didn't blow me away.

Like the book, this movie is about love, hope, and the importance of family. Charlie is the hero. He lives on the poor side of town with one wish. All he wants is to win a golden ticket and tour the Wonka chocolate factory. All the other ticket holders have everything they've ever wanted. Not Charlie. All he has is a loving family. But he's soon going to have so much more.

My problems with the movie start with the lead character of Willy Wonka. In the book, Wonka is a strange character, no question about that. But in the movie, Johnny Depp plays him as downright weird. He's not really funny or goofy, just peculiar. He has a haircut like my grandmother's, purplish eyes, and is as pale as a ghost. His voice is high and he seems to be afraid of germs. In the book, Willy Wonka may not have been an average guy, but he wasn't a freak. I didn't like Depp's performance at all. It left me cold.

The reviewer identifies one of the film's weaknesses: the portrayal of Willy Wonka by Johnny Depp.

I also didn't like what the director did to the Oompa-Loompas. Why did they all have to look alike? The males and females, young and old, all have just one face. What's the point of that? I think they would have been a lot more interesting to watch if they all had different faces, like the Munchkins in *The Wizard of Oz*. It's Burton's fault for not thinking this through.

But I have to say that the rest of the casting is brilliant, especially Freddie Highmore, who plays Charlie Bucket. He's young and yet he delivers a five-star performance. He's a good kid and has a twinkle in his eye the whole time. You can tell he's so excited just to be inside Wonka's chocolate factory. The parents are also lovable and some of the grandparents are very **spunky**.

The other golden ticket winners are also **terrific**. The screenwriters wrote additional scenes for us to see Augustus, Veruca, Violet, and Mike Teavee in action. That was a smart move. The actors who play these characters are unforgettable and make the most of their time on camera.

The screenwriters added two other subplots, but I think they're lame. The first one involves Wonka's dad, who is a **dentist**. When Willy was a boy, his father wouldn't let him have any candy and made his son wear the biggest set of braces ever made. These scenes are supposed to explain why Wonka had to leave home and live out his dream of having candy all the time. But the dental scenes are just creepy and a little scary. Plus, who cares why Wonka grew to love candy? Who doesn't love candy?

The reviewer finds the rest of the casting to be a strength of the movie. Reviews usually include comments about the actors as well as the pacing and special effects.

The reviewer makes judgments that compare the movie with the book.

The second subplot also relates to Wonka's childhood. Why won't Wonka let Charlie's family come along to the chocolate factory? It's because Wonka had a bad relationship with his own dad. So he doesn't think much about family.

What else do these subplots show? To me, they prove that Willy Wonka still has to grow up. He has to deal with his dad, and both of them have to learn how to forgive and forget. In the end, Charlie proves that he's much more mature than Wonka.

On the plus side, the movie was very colorful. Kids will love the story of Charlie, and they'll enjoy the songs that the Oompa-Loompas sing. On the other hand, adults may feel that the movie is just too strange. Maybe a different director should try to make a better version of this classic story.

The reviewer identifies the audience for the movie and concludes that another director might have done a better job adapting the book to the big screen.

Understand the Reviews

- What book and movie are reviewed?
- Look at the book review of *Charlie and the Chocolate Factory*. Does the critic like the book? How can you tell?
- What does the critic think you can learn from reading *Charlie and the Chocolate Factory*?
- Look at the movie review of *Charlie and the Chocolate Factory*. Does the critic like the book or the movie better? How can you tell?

Focus on Comprehension: Compare and Contrast

- How is Charlie different from the other contest winners?
- On page 22, the critic compares the book and the movie. What are some similarities?
- On page 24, the critic mentions the Oompa-Loompas. She says they all look the same. Then she compares them with characters from another movie. What is the other movie?

Focus on Including Questions

Many critics include questions in their articles because they make readers stop and think while they are reading. Identify places in the text where the critic included questions. What do those questions make you think about?

Analyze the Tools Writers Use: Writer's Voice

- On page 20, the critic describes the contest winners. What do you visualize when you read these short descriptions?
- On page 20, the critic says that Charlie is a good kid—too good to be true. What does this tell you about the critic?
- At the end of the review, the critic says that in real life, there are no golden tickets. Does this mean the critic is optimistic, pessimistic, or pragmatic?

Focus on Words: Suffixes

Make a chart like the one below. For each word, identify its part of speech. Then identify the base or root word and suffix. Finally, identify the word's meaning.

Page	Word	Part of Speech	Base or Root Word	Suffix	Definition
20	obnoxious				
20	sympathize				
20	optimistic				
24	spunky				
24	terrific				
24	dentist				

How does a critic write a review of a book and a review of a movie based on a book?

Reread "Charlie the Champ!" and "Charlie Is Way, Way Over the Top" and think about what Cynthia Swain did to put these reviews together.

1. Choose a Book and a Movie Based on the Book

Identify the title, author, and when the book was published. For instance, this review was about a book published in 1964. In a review of a movie based on a book, the critic must also identify the book, tell the title of the movie and when it debuted, or was first shown. For example, this review was about a movie from 2005.

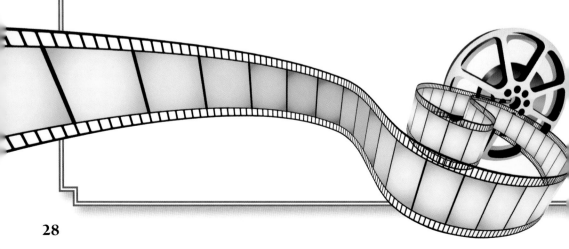

Identify the Audience for the Reviews

Reviewers should let readers know who might like the book and the movie, and who might not like it. In the last paragraph of the book review, the critic says that readers will enjoy "Dahl's magic." In the movie review, the critic states that kids "will love the story of Charlie, and they'll enjoy the songs that the Oompa-Loompas sing." Kids will probably enjoy the movie more than parents will because "adults may feel that the movie is just too strange."

Provide a Brief Summary

Critics tell readers what the book or movie is about, but they shouldn't give away every detail!

4. Identify and Give Examples of Strengths and Weaknesses

Reviewers tell about the strengths and weaknesses. They offer judgments on those strengths and weaknesses and support their judgments with evidence from the book and movie. Remember that critics put their own voices into the reviews.

Strengths of Book	Supporting Evidence
description of details	". . . his imagination is still spectacular. I loved his description of the factory's chocolate river with funnels to make fudge."
supporting characters	"And nothing is more fantastic than the tribe of the Oompa-Loompas."

Weaknesses	Supporting Evidence
main character, Charlie Bucket	"It's hard not to sympathize with Charlie, but I have to admit I found him a little too good to be true."

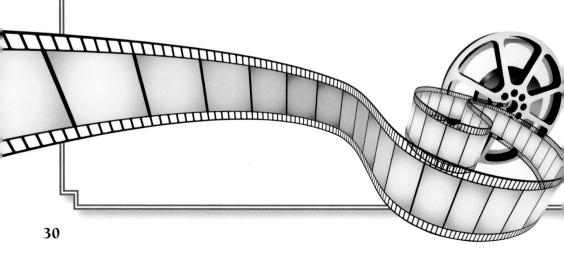

Strengths of Movie	Supporting Evidence
most casting choices	". . . the rest of the casting is brilliant, especially Freddie Highmore, who plays Charlie Bucket. He's young and yet he delivers a five-star performance."
expanding the roles of the other golden ticket winners	"The screenwriters wrote additional scenes for us to see Augustus, Veruca, Violet, and Mike Teavee in action. That was a smart move."

Weaknesses	Supporting Evidence
Oompa-Loompas portrayal	"I also didn't like what the director did to the Oompa-Loompas. Why did they all have to look alike?"

5. Write a Conclusion

Include a statement or question expressing what you think about the book or film.

Glossary

abusive   (uh-BYOO-siv) hurtful (page 12)

bravery   (BRAY-vuh-ree) fearlessness (page 10)

childhood   (CHILD-hood) youth (page 12)

dentist   (DEN-tist) a doctor who fixes teeth (page 24)

dramatizes   (DRAH-muh-tize-es) makes something seem more important (page 12)

hilarious   (hih-LAIR-ee-us) very funny (page 12)

obnoxious   (ahb-NAHK-shus) offensive (page 20)

optimistic   (ahp-tih-MIS-tik) hopeful (page 20)

sarcastic   (sar-KAS-tik) mean-spirited (page 10)

spunky   (SPUN-kee) lively (page 24)

sympathize   (SIM-puh-thize) pity (page 20)

terrific   (tuh-RIH-fik) great (page 24)

terrify   (TAIR-ih-fy) scare (page 9)